Felipe's Journey

by Susan Schott Karr

When Felipe woke up, he lay in bed for a few minutes with his eyes closed. He liked to pretend he was still in his old home in Bello, Colombia. Mama's voice calling him for breakfast was the same. But the sound of children playing soccer in the park next door was missing.

Felipe sat up and looked out the window. Now he knew for sure he was no longer in Colombia. He was in Tampa, Florida. He could only see buildings in the distance, not mountains.

One week earlier, Felipe's family had moved to the United States to open a restaurant. His father spent all day trying out new recipes while workers fixed up the restaurant. At least the smells of hen stew and coconut rice were familiar!

Felipe had a cousin named Paula in Tampa who had moved to the United States with her family a year ago. She was going to teach him English, and today was his first lesson.

Paula started by teaching Felipe words for things he would need in class, like books, pencils, and other school supplies. When it was time for a break, they watched TV. Felipe's favorite sport was on! "What is the English word for *fútbol*?" he asked.

"It's called soccer," Paula replied. "Here, football is a different game with different rules."

Felipe practiced saying *soccer*. "Teach me more!" he said.

3

The summer sped by, and Felipe continued to learn. Papa's restaurant opened and was a success! But Felipe still missed playing soccer with his friends.

On the first day of school, Felipe could understand almost everything the teacher said. When it was time for recess, Felipe approached a girl and asked quietly, "Do you play soccer?"

"It's our favorite game!" the girl replied. She led Felipe to the playground, where a small group was already playing soccer! Another student kicked the ball to Felipe and shouted, "Want to play?"

"Yes!" Felipe said, kicking the ball toward the crowd of his cheering new friends.